Our Butterfly Blessings
Personal Journal of Healing Peace, Love and Hope After Suicide

Sharon Gorker Norris

Sharon Gorker Norris
Copyright © 2006 Sharon Gorker Norris
All rights reserved.
The cover design and watercolor were created by artist Clint Metcalf.
ISBN 1-4196-3176-4
ISBN-13: 978-1419631764

To order additional copies, please use these websites:
www.ourbutterflyblessings.com and Amazon.com

Dedication

This book is especially dedicated to our beloved son, Ryan John Norris. Even though he is beyond our embrace, he has continued to bless our lives through the symbols of butterflies. Also, to my loving husband Larry, our precious daughter Kamie, her devoted husband Josh, and our perfect granddaughters Cali Ryanna and Bayli Jaron. In addition, I would like to dedicate this book to all of our extended family and friends who love Ryan and help us keep his spirit alive.

Cover Picture

The butterflies on the front cover were drawn by Ryan John when he was 12 years old. He drew them right before he took his butterfly collection down from his bedroom wall. These butterflies were the only original drawings we found in his art collection. His favorite form of art was pen and ink.

Acknowledgements

    I would like to personally thank our daughter Kamie Norris, my mother Virginia Gorker, and our friends Brett Simpson, Ruth Ann Siebert and Dr. Gary Noel Ross for giving their time to help me transform my journal into a manuscript. I also want to especially thank my loving husband Larry for encouraging me to follow my dreams and have my manuscript printed.

Foreword

The butterfly garden in the Norris' backyard kept expanding. New butterflies came each season as new plants and flowers were added. The garden enriched the entire community -- that is the nature of butterflies. They spread the joy of flowers wherever they flew.

Such joy brings healing to the earth and its inhabitants. This witness of God's healing power has expanded through "Our Butterfly Blessings," Sharon Norris' powerful affirmation of the power of love to heal life's deepest pain.

When their son Ryan died, Sharon and Larry, and their daughter Kamie, were distraught. But in the midst of their grief, they found a symbol to comfort and sustain them. Their journey brings Ryan closer to them and to others who share their story.

Theologian Paul Tillich wrote that one of the characteristics of a symbol "is that it opens up levels of reality which otherwise are closed for us." Certainly, the butterflies for the Norris family opened them, and now us, to a new reality of healing and hope.

I am grateful to be one of those whose life is continually blessed by this witness and the ministry of the Norris family's story.

Barbara Howard

Barbara Howard was born in Mobile, Alabama, and lives in Independence, Missouri. She has a B.A. from Graceland College and has done graduate work at Saint Paul School of Theology, University of Missouri at Kansas City, and Kansas University. She has been an editor for Herald House and has written numerous articles and several books. She compiled Children: Of Such Is the Kingdom (1979) in observance of the International Year of the Child. Barbara frequently leads retreats and workshops with her husband, Richard.

Table of Contents

Our Story 1

Why Butterflies? 7

Kamie's Great Spangled Fritillary 9

Our Monarch 11

My Clouded Sulfur 13

Larry's Clouded Sulfur 15

Our Symbolic Butterflies 17

Nathan's Butterflies 19

My School Butterfly 21

The Injured Butterfly 23

Butterfly Gifts of Love from Others 25

My Garden Butterfly 27

Tagging and Raising Monarchs 29

The Butterfly Garden's Blessing 33

Butterfly World 35

Our Expanded Butterfly Garden 37
Butterfly Festival 39
Monarch Migration 41
A Butterfly Etched in Glass 43
My Personal Metamorphosis 47
My Confirmation Butterfly 51
Out of the Darkness 53
Epilogue 57
Recognizing Depression 59

Photo by Pat Carver

Our Story

On August 17, 1993, our 20-year-old son, Ryan John, took his own life while in the depths of depression. Ryan was seeking professional help for his illness when his pain consumed him. Time was not allowed to help heal him on earth.

My husband Larry and I were married in 1970. Larry has always been my true love, and my best friend. He has worked full-time as a minister in our church since 1980. I am a music teacher and a lay minister, but my favorite job has always been being "Mom" -- and now even "Grandma"! Ryan was the firstborn of our two children. His sister, Kamie, is two years younger, and she always adored him. Our children made our family dreams come true. When Ryan took his own life, those dreams were shattered, and our lives were forever changed.

I miss our son's handsome face, his voice, his friendship, his mischievous smile, his witty personality, and his great sense of humor (he could always make me laugh at anything). I miss his gift of art, his perfectionism, his sensitivity, his stubbornness, his love for weight lifting, and his strong embrace.

Ryan was never really diagnosed, but we believe he must have been bipolar. Our problem was that his illness was not obvious. He didn't want to worry us with his feelings of sadness, worthlessness, and failure. We thought his mood swings and low grades in high school were just part of adolescence. We didn't even know the signs of depression.

Ryan's grades improved markedly when he went to college. He loved college life and seemed to be doing great. Ryan knew he wanted to major in education, and his course work was going well. He had a nice car, lots of friends, and was dating the girl of his dreams. He knew he should have been happy, but he wasn't, and didn't understand why. He kept his innermost feelings from even his best friends. We didn't know the significance of his struggles until a few weeks before he took his life.

Ryan had finished his sophomore year at college, and was renting a home with two of his best friends while working during the summer. His first two jobs had fallen through, and during his third job Ryan's spirits broke in a way that made us notice that something was terribly wrong. His countenance was sad and his body was slumped. We had never seen him like that before. I told him I thought he should see someone who could talk to him about the way he was feeling, but he assured me that everything was under control. He said he had been through this before, and had always pulled himself out of it.

Larry had to go out of town for the next couple of days, and before he left, Ryan promised us he was fine. But while Larry was gone, Ryan tried to hang himself in his own home. He had managed to free himself, and actually drove straight home to me. He began crying on my shoulder and saying I was right, he did need help. Things had gotten out of control this time. As I looked at him closely, I saw marks on his neck. His suicide note was crumpled in his hand. He was beyond merely talking to someone for help. I immediately called a psychologist and was told to take him to a hospital where he would be under suicide watch. Larry came straight home, and we had Ryan moved to what we believed was the best facility for the treatment of depression in our area.

Ryan had been in the hospital for only 20 days when he said that he was ready to go home with us. We didn't feel right about him going home that soon, but the doctor assured us that Ryan would be fine. He told us that Ryan should continue to take his medicine; however, the doctor never warned us to watch Ryan closely. We didn't have a clue that he could still be considering suicide.

After we brought Ryan home, we were even more convinced that he wasn't yet well. We called the doctor frequently, and had set up an early follow-up visit. Ryan had been home for only six days when he bought a shotgun and ended his life in the nearby woods. He never made it to his follow-up visit.

Ryan kept his pain to himself. We never knew about his suffering until we could actually see it. But even then, we didn't understand it. One of the things we learned while Ryan was in the hospital was that he felt like he had been a failure his whole life, and was just floating along without a purpose. Everyone feels that way sometimes, but the illness made it life-threatening for him.

It is important for us to teach others to recognize the signs of depression, because we didn't know them until it was too late. I know without a doubt that Ryan wants us to be helping others now. I believe that with more time, Ryan could have been helped, and would still be with us today. I wish we could help erase the stigma of mental illness. Recent studies have shown that over one-third of Americans suffer from depression in some form during their lifetime. Depression is a serious illness, like cancer or heart disease, and should be treated.

Eighty percent of those suffering could be treated successfully, but only twenty percent will seek professional help and find healing peace in recovery.

We will forever treasure the memories of Ryan's precious life on earth with us. We truly ache for his embrace. No one can take his place in our hearts. Our family's grief has been bearable only by knowing that Ryan is now free from his pain and despair, and at peace with our Lord.

No one could have been more blessed by God after the death of a child than we were through family and friends and their gifts of love. God works to bless us all in many different ways, sometimes mysteriously. For our family, blessings even come through butterflies.

Why Butterflies?

Ryan first started chasing butterflies with his very own net around the age of five, when we lived in Lawrence, Kansas. He loved running to catch them, and acquired quite an assorted, colorful collection. His enthusiasm for the butterflies gave joy to both Ryan and me.

When we moved to St. Louis, Missouri, Ryan continued his love for butterflies. I will never forget how beautifully he drew butterfly pictures for one of our favorite books, Hope for the Flowers by Trina Paulus. Our family used his pictures for an Easter service to illustrate the Resurrection.

Memories of Ryan running through an open field to catch butterflies behind our home in Mt. Pleasant, Michigan bring a smile to those who knew and loved him. He framed his butterflies and displayed them on his bedroom wall. But when Ryan was 12 years old, he lost interest in them and tucked them away.

Eight years later, exactly one day after Ryan's death, we came across a small cardboard box in his top dresser drawer. Inside were five remaining butterflies from his original collection -- probably his favorites. They were still in perfect condition. We chose to display them in a beveled glass box.

During the course of the next three days, Larry, Kamie and I were blessed mysteriously by the presence of live butterflies exactly like the few that remained of Ryan's collection. These were the beginning of countless treasured butterfly blessings that continually touch our lives.

Photo by Dr. Gary Noel Ross

Kamie's Great Spangled Fritillary

    The first butterfly blessing came to Kamie, on the night of the funeral home visitation for Ryan, August 18, 1993. Our extended family was in our home sharing treasured memories of Ryan. Kamie walked into our living room and said, "There is a butterfly on our back deck that will not go away." Larry and I immediately followed her to the deck. I expected to see a moth rather than a butterfly, since it was very late at night. But there on the table where Kamie had been sitting was a beautiful orange, black and silver-speckled butterfly. (We now know it to be the Great Spangled Fritillary). Kamie nudged the butterfly several times, and it slowly crawled onto her finger. She took it to the edge of the deck and shook her hand to get it to fly away. After a few more nudges, the butterfly flew into the darkness as Kamie called out, "Go free!"

    We wanted Ryan to still be with us on this earth. We knew we would always miss him, but the butterfly helped us to know that Ryan's suffering had ended. We felt as though Ryan's spirit had come to Kamie through that special butterfly, so all of us would know that he was free from his despair and at peace with the Lord.

Our Monarch

The next day, August 19, was the day of Ryan's memorial service at our church in Lawrence, Kansas. The second butterfly blessing came as we were walking through the parking lot to the church. Kamie was walking just ahead of Larry and me. Our eyes followed her as she stopped to look at a beautiful orange and black butterfly that was right in our path. When we looked closer, we noticed that the butterfly -- a Monarch -- was wounded and unable to fly. Kamie reached down, picked it up gently, and placed it in a safe grassy area.

We felt like this was a special sign. Ryan had been wounded. He was physically gone, but his spirit remained with us through that beautiful butterfly. Our second butterfly blessing was sent with love.

Photo by Dr. Gary Noel Ross

My Clouded Sulfur

On the morning of August 20, following Ryan's memorial service and burial, I was in the depths of my grief. I guess the numbness was wearing off. I had cried hysterically in Larry's arms for an hour and a half. Afterward, I spoke in my heart to Ryan, telling him that I needed a sign of my very own that day to know he was okay.

Later that morning, as I was standing on our front porch, a small yellow butterfly came to drink nectar from the flowers in the large barrel next to me. Years before, I had been given spiritual experiences with light, so I assumed that I would receive my sign from Ryan in that way. But as I moved closer to the butterfly and held out my hand, I knew the butterfly was my personal sign.

The yellow butterfly (a Clouded Sulfur) flew boldly around my open, outstretched hand several times. I could have easily caught it to keep forever, but was reminded of what a friend, David Glauner had shared with us the evening before. He had said, "Corrie Ten Boom tells us we need to always love our children with an open hand, and not to hold them too tightly."

Tearfully, I called out to Larry. After he joined me on the porch, the butterfly stayed close to us for several minutes. It flew off and returned to us three times. When it was finally gone, Larry whispered to me, "He just doesn't want to leave us." In my own heart, I knew for certain that Ryan was indeed okay, and I was now prepared to symbolically let him go free. When I went inside the house and shared this marvelous experience with my sister-in-law Carol Vincent, she said my butterfly was yellow because yellow is the color of light.

It was the sign I had asked for that morning! I was given the spirit of peace through that butterfly of light.

Photo by Dr. Gary Noel Ross

Larry's Clouded Sulfur

The very same day of my special butterfly blessing, Larry also received his. We were driving my parent's station wagon to the cemetery, taking more of the fresh flowers that had come to our home in memory of Ryan. Larry was driving. Suddenly, a Clouded Sulfur, exactly like the one we had seen on our porch, flew up against the windshield in front of Larry. Even though the car was going around 40 m.p.h., the butterfly seemed to be at a standstill. It appeared to be looking right into Larry's eyes. Then, as if that wasn't enough to believe, the butterfly flew to Larry's side window and followed along for a while before flying away. Our eyes brimmed with tears, and we knew instantly that the butterfly was Larry's blessing from Ryan.

Our Symbolic Butterflies

Kamie, Larry, and I had been, individually and collectively, blessed by the special presence of a butterfly following Ryan's death. That alone would have been enough for us, but the blessings continued.

Shortly after our personal butterfly experiences, I looked more closely at Ryan's old collection. I simply couldn't believe what I noticed this time. The collection consisted of two Monarchs, one Great Spangled Fritillary, one small Clouded Sulfur, and a Black Swallowtail. Each of us had been blessed by the presence of living butterflies exactly like those Ryan had saved. What a beautiful, joyful visualization of the hope of the Resurrection for us.

I couldn't help wondering why the Black Swallowtail hadn't come to one of us. Then the answer came to my mind and heart: Ryan hadn't caught the Swallowtail. Craig Hunter, a college friend of ours who also collected butterflies, had given it to Ryan one summer while we were on vacation. Knowing that made our personal experiences even more of a blessing for us!

Photo by Dr. Gary Noel Ross

Nathan's Butterflies

Our next butterfly blessing came to us through our nephew Nathan Butler, my sister Sue Gorker's son. They lived nearby and he had been, in many ways, like a little brother to Ryan and Kamie. Nathan's experience happened the same day as Larry's and mine, before he had heard about ours.

That evening, Sue and Nathan came to our home to bring us one of her many "butterfly gifts of love," and especially to have Nathan share his story with us. I couldn't believe the excitement in Nathan's voice as he said, "When I got out of the car today, a yellow butterfly came up to me and started flying all around me, like it wanted to play." Sue said it actually reminded her of the times Ryan and Nathan wrestled together. Nathan continued, "The butterfly started to fly off, so I chased it to the backyard. It led me to a huge Monarch with many small butterflies flying around it."

My heart was overflowing. I immediately gave Nathan a big hug. As a mother, it was of great concern for me to know that Ryan wasn't lonely. Now I felt reassured that Ryan was not only with our Lord, but many loved ones were there with him. He was not alone! I picture those butterflies often in my mind.

Photo by Dr. Gary Noel Ross

My School Butterfly

    Two weeks after Ryan's death, the new school year started and I had to begin teaching. Needless to say, my heart was not in going back to work. I had been hired earlier that summer to teach vocal music in a brand-new elementary school. Due to our tragedy, all excitement for my job was gone. At the end of the first week, there was to be an outside dedication ceremony at the school. I was expected to lead the students in their new pep song.

    I was really dreading having to be in front of the entire school. I didn't know how I was going to be able to show enthusiasm for the students. During the dedication, just before it was time for me to lead the singing, a yellow butterfly flew right across the stage where I would be standing. It didn't stay, but flew gently away and out of sight. It was exactly what I needed at that moment. The presence of that butterfly gave me the joy and energy to stand before the school and lead everyone in song.

    Before Ryan's death, he had decided to be an elementary school teacher. When I saw the butterfly, I felt that Ryan was letting me know he was there with me -- in my job, where I needed to be. Another blessing of love!

Photo by Larry Waddell

The Injured Butterfly

    Our nephew Larry Waddell, my husband's namesake, is a professional photographer with many other talents and skills. During the summer of Ryan's death, Larry had taken a photo of a beautiful yellow Swallowtail near the Boundary Waters. He had planned to put it in a show he was having that fall. After inspecting the photo closely, Larry was very disappointed to discover that the butterfly was injured. He filed the photo, with no intention of ever using it.

    Several weeks later, after Ryan's memorial and hearing about our butterfly experiences, Larry was reminded of the Swallowtail photo he had filed away. He had the photo enlarged and prepared it to be among the photographs in his show. Larry titled the photo "Ryan," and received more positive responses from it than any of his other photos. We believe it was taken especially for us.

Butterfly Gifts of Love from Others

    We have received many gifts of love in Ryan's memory from family and friends. Each gift is very special to us. Every room in our home has several beautiful butterflies, in a variety of different art forms. How comforting it is to have each one within view. Assorted flower seeds and bushes to attract butterflies were given to us by two families we are close to, the Becketts and the Simpsons. We've been friends since our college days, and our children grew up together.

    Our nephew, Larry, sent us picture plans for a large, cedar butterfly house. My father, John Gorker, built it with his skilled hands and set it on a pole in our backyard. A brass plaque on it reads, "In Memory of Ryan's New Life with the Lord."

    The first spring after Ryan's death, my father helped me plant a small rectangular garden around the butterfly house. I filled it with the flower seeds and butterfly bushes, and placed a birdbath on the ground inside it for the butterflies to drink from. I also placed several large stones among the flowers where the butterflies could dry the morning dew from their wings. My mother gave us a colorful nectar feeder as an extra treat for the butterflies. Two of Ryan's best friends, Dave and Marcy Black, gave us a sign for the garden that reads, "Butterfly Crossing."

    Somehow, creating the garden and watching it grow helped our grieving process. What a blessing it was for us to sit and feel God's peace as we watched the wonder and beauty of nature, and to experience the hope of butterflies in our own backyard.

Photo by Dr. Gary Noel Ross

My Garden Butterfly

On August 17, 1994, one year after his death, I woke up asking for another special sign from Ryan. I went to the butterfly garden that morning to water it. As I was collecting the garden hose, a big, beautiful yellow butterfly flew right into the middle of the garden. It didn't leave, but when I came back with my camera, I couldn't find it anywhere. I searched for at least ten minutes, then gave up and went back to get the hose.

In the very spot where I released the first spray of water, the butterfly came out and flew away, right before my eyes. It had been there, in front of me, the entire time I was looking for it.

I immediately knew this experience was telling me that Ryan is always near us, even though we can't see him. Again, I praised God for Ryan and our butterfly blessings!

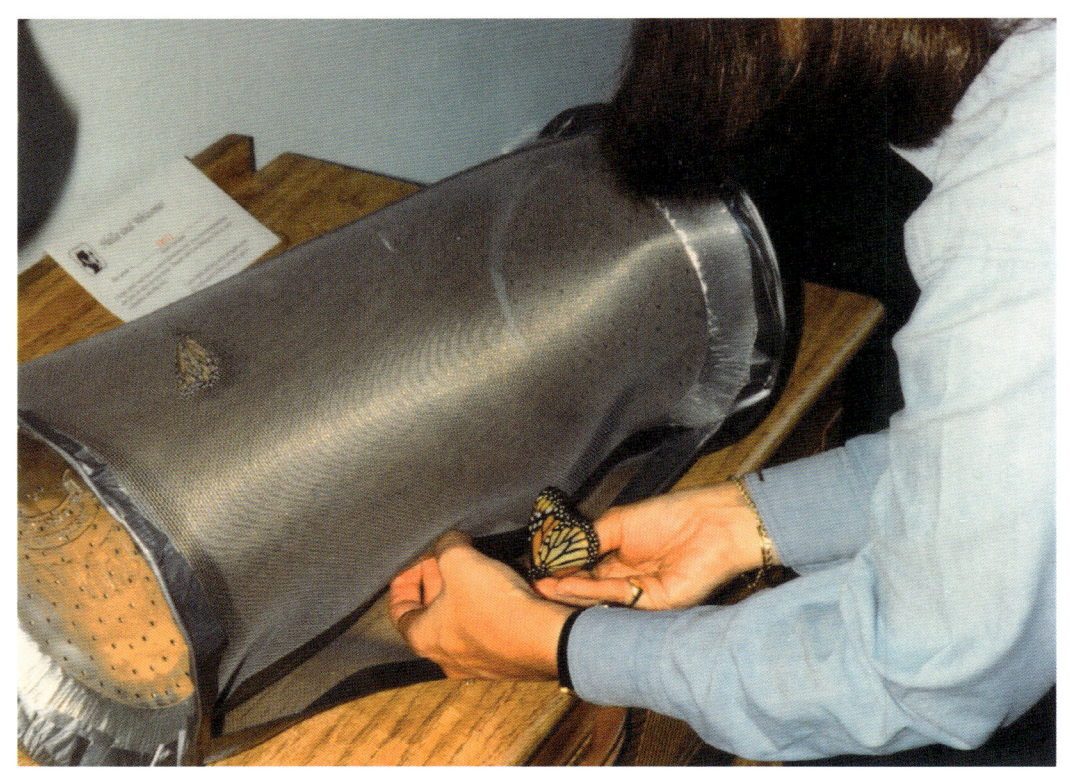

Tagging and Raising Monarchs

In September of 1994, I was invited to "tag" Monarchs with a long-time friend, Karen DeVictor, from Lawrence, Kansas. We had been next-door neighbors when our children were young. Karen knew I would enjoy tagging Monarchs with her, as she was aware of how much butterflies had come to mean to our family since Ryan's death.

The tagging is a system that the Kansas University Science/Biology Department uses to document the migration of Monarchs to Mexico each year. After catching the Monarchs with our nets, we placed them in a large screen cage. We then took them out, one by one, and wrote down information about them. We measured their wings, identified them as male or female, and wrote down the weather conditions, the time and date, and the place or plant where they were caught. Then we glued a tiny colored and numbered, tissue-thin tag to the bottom wing of each butterfly. We fed them sugar water until the tags were dry. Our last task was to release them for their continued journey to Mexico. It was a joy to hold them, study them up close, and release them to freedom.

While tagging the Monarchs, Karen told me that K.U. also sold kits for people to raise their own Monarchs to release. I could hardly wait to get home and order my kit. In a few short weeks, I was able to experience the miracle of actually watching my own Monarchs grow -- from the larvae stage, through making their own chrysalis, to turning themselves into incredibly beautiful butterflies. What a sight!

My first two butterflies emerged while Larry and I were on a short vacation in the Ozarks. We had taken their chrysalis with us in a screen cage because we knew they were close to breaking out. Sure enough, when we returned to our motel room one evening, we found two newly emerged female butterflies hanging from the top of the cage and drying their perfect wings.

We brought the butterflies back home with us so Kamie could see them before we released them. The next morning, we fed them sugar water and put them on a butterfly bush in a sunny spot. On my way to school, I prayed for their safe journey to Mexico. As I was praying, the song "Ride Like the Wind" came on the radio. When I heard the lyric, "…got such a long ways to go, to make it to the border of Mexico," I knew that, without a doubt, my butterflies were going to complete their trip safe and sound.

The Butterfly Garden's Blessing

    Several times in my life, I have been blessed with special signs from God through the miracle of light. The following experience with our butterfly garden happened near the end of the fall of 1994, the first year of our garden.

    One morning before school, I walked onto the back deck to look at the garden. I couldn't believe how it glowed. I gazed up and saw that the sky was very cloudy, but one shaft of light was shining down directly over the garden. Everything else was dark. It was spectacular! I immediately ran for my camera. I was afraid the light would be gone by the time I returned, but I had to try to capture the beauty so I could share it with others. When I returned the light was still there, and the result was a breathtaking photo verifying this miracle.

    This light made me feel extremely warm inside, because I knew that God was aware of how special the garden was to me. The flowers were near the end of their beauty for the season, and I felt as if God was showering a final blessing on our memorial garden to Ryan.

    The butterfly house, the flowers, and all the butterflies that had been part of our lives throughout that year brought a healing power to my grieving process. I will think of their beauty year after year for the rest of my life. Nature has such a powerful message of peace, love and hope.

Butterfly World

In the spring of 1995, Larry and I celebrated our 25th wedding anniversary with a cruise to the Bahamas, including two extra days in Miami before flying back home. Larry surprised me with a special visit to Butterfly World in Coconut Creek, Florida. What a dream come true!

Butterfly World was the first of its kind in the U.S. and, at the time, was considered to be the largest in the world. We spent four hours there, watching many kinds of butterflies fly around us. Several of them landed right on Larry. One reason we stayed so long was my wish for one to land on me voluntarily.

I was sitting patiently on a bench when an employee came to me and asked if I would like to hold a butterfly. She said they didn't normally encourage visitors to touch the butterflies, but she realized I had been there a long time, and she knew of one that was wounded and wouldn't live much longer. I was thrilled when she brought me a large, iridescent blue Morpho. It was beautiful, but wounded, and of course it reminded me of Ryan. Tears blurred my eyes immediately. A short time later, it flew from my hand, and a different butterfly actually landed near my heart. Soon, another one voluntarily rested on my outstretched hand for me to enjoy before it flew off again.

I was then able to leave Butterfly World, feeling very blessed once again by God's frail winged creatures of beauty. Through them, I felt the peace of Ryan's presence near me.

Our Extended Garden

Larry and I dreamed about enlarging our garden and decided to put our plans into action. In the spring of 1996, Larry prepared the ground, and a flower seed company came and planted a mixture of perennial wildflowers the full width of the bottom of our backyard. The woods behind it created a gorgeous backdrop. We patiently watched the seeds grow into beautiful flowers, which attracted more and more butterflies to our backyard. It was a perfect natural habitat.

The very first spring day that Larry, Kamie, our granddaughter Cali Ryanna, and I were on our back patio together, each one of us was blessed. While looking at our newly planted garden, we all watched a bright yellow Sulfur, and then a large Monarch, fly gracefully across the full length of the garden. What a thrill it was to see Cali pointing excitedly toward the butterflies. They were the first I had noticed in our yard that spring.

I sensed that Ryan was letting us know he was aware of our new, extended garden made in his memory, and it would be continually blessed with many butterflies from heaven. Reflecting on the garden, our new butterflies that spring, and our angelic granddaughter, I was reminded with joy that life does go on. I thank God for his eternal blessings of hope.

Butterfly Festival

    The weekend of August 16-17, 1997 was exactly four years after Ryan's death. Larry and I were delighted to learn that Powell Gardens, a nearby public garden, was having its very first "Butterfly Festival." We felt that the festival was meant especially for us and were excited to attend, knowing that we would be blessed!

    We walked through an enclosed, mist-filled garden for butterflies, but the highlight for us was the classes by Dr. Gary Noel Ross that we attended. We were drawn to him with awe because of his outstanding knowledge and obvious passion for butterflies. Our favorite of his classes was "The Mythological, Cultural, and Spiritual Aspects of Butterflies."

    We were fascinated to learn that the Greek word for butterfly is "psyche" -- the same as the Greek word for "soul" -- and that many people in this world believe butterflies actually carry the spirits of our dead. Dr. Ross also shared many stories that confirmed our own butterfly experiences since Ryan's death.

    We shared our story about Ryan with Dr. Ross personally, and he has since shared some of our experiences with others. We have kept in touch and continue to enjoy our friendship. Sharing our story with others helps lessen our own pain, and we realize that by sharing our blessings others may be helped to find joy.

Monarch Migration

Larry and I were invited to participate in a weekend church conference held in San Diego, California in November of 1997. That weekend, we shared our story about Ryan, as well as some of our butterfly blessings.

Following the conference, we were able to vacation up the coast and witness the migration of the Monarchs that live west of the Rocky Mountains. What an awesome sight! It was like nothing I had ever experienced. We observed thousands of beautiful Monarchs resting together in trees of refuge, as part of their long journey. They remain there through the winter months before continuing their journey in the spring. The Monarchs then fly to find a mate to continue their life cycle, and soon die. The new generation grows and begins the entire journey all over again. It is like a miracle to me that every year the new generation of Monarchs knows the exact trees for migration each winter.

The symbolism of the Monarch's life is remarkable. I think of it as another tangible sign from God that all life is important and has a purpose. Like the Monarch, our own circle of life goes on and on. I also believe our life on earth is just one part of our journey of "Eternal Life."

Photo by Jim Hannah

A Butterfly Etched In Glass

Larry and I celebrated our 30th wedding anniversary in 2000. We vacationed in Victoria and spent several days driving through the rain forests of Washington. It was wonderful seeing butterflies in the beauty of God's nature.

The following week, we were guests at a church family camp near Seattle. We openly shared our personal journeys of grief after Ryan's tragic death, and also shared our butterfly experiences of peace, love, and hope.

A man named Bob Evans later told us that at first he had felt sorry for us. He truly believed that Ryan was alone -- and not with our Lord -- because of the way he had died. Bob said he was interested in our experiences, but couldn't really accept them because of the teachings from his childhood. Near the end of the week, he had a change of heart.

We were all participating in a service where we were asked to pick out a small piece of broken colored glass, which represented our life. We were then asked to glue it onto a large framed piece of clear glass. The end product became a lovely, multicolored stained glass window, which represented all our lives blended beautifully together.

Bob later told us that something urged him to go back to the table after the service, and to pick up an unused piece of glass for himself. He said he didn't even look them over this time; he just immediately picked one up, as though drawn to it. When he looked at it closely, he saw that etched into the small round piece of glass was a tiny butterfly. Bob said he instantly felt that our butterfly experiences were true, and that Ryan was indeed with our Lord.

When Bob shared this with us, he handed me that small piece of etched glass and said he wanted me to keep it. I told him I felt his testimony could someday help others who might also believe the same way he had. Bob is a changed man, and has taken many opportunities to share our Lord's love with others. Butterflies have also become very special to him since that experience.

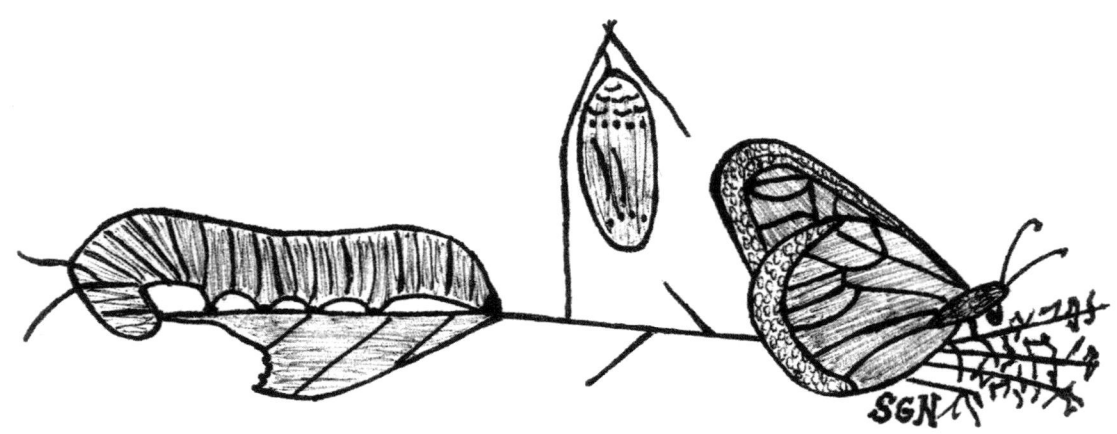

My Personal Metamorphosis

The metamorphosis of butterflies has always fascinated me. I've especially enjoyed watching a Monarch's mysterious change from a tiny, wiggly caterpillar to a bright green chrysalis, which later breaks open to free a beautiful, delicate-winged butterfly. What a transformation!

My life seems to have slowly gone through a metamorphosis of its own. I had been richly blessed with a wonderful family, especially my husband and our two precious children. Later came our perfect granddaughter Cali, our wonderful son-in-law Josh, and our second perfect granddaughter Bayli. As a teacher and a lay minister, I have also been blessed daily by people from different walks of life.

Our story is tragic because we didn't know or recognize the signs of Ryan's depression. He didn't want to worry us with his personal struggles, and he hid them well. By the time we found out, Ryan was already "severely" depressed. There was not enough time for the medication and treatment to take effect before he chose a permanent solution to end what may have been a temporary problem. All he was capable of thinking about was ending his pain.

Since Ryan's death, Larry and I have both shared our experience with many people. We try to help educate young and old about the signs of depression, and to let those presently suffering know that life can get better. I have shared Ryan's story in schools at PTA meetings, in classroom settings, and in teacher workshops. Larry and I continue to share at church congregations, weekend retreats, and youth and family camps locally, nationally and internationally. We speak with many people individually. We listen and share our story as suicide survivors, not as professionals.

My personal desire to help others who suffer in the way Ryan did changed to a passion for me in the spring of 1998. While sharing with two high school students who were struggling with depression, I felt the "call" to search for new avenues to reach out to others suffering from depression. It was the first time I had felt such energy since Ryan's death.

That feeling was soon confirmed when I shared it with a new friend, Richard Gillard, who had started support groups for suicide prevention and survivors in Australia. His work touched my heart deeply. I don't think the timing of our acquaintance was merely a coincidence. I can almost say it was another "butterfly blessing," because the logo for his support groups was a butterfly.

I felt like I had started a new phase of my personal metamorphosis. I soon had the opportunity to be instrumental in helping set up a suicide prevention program in the school district where I taught. It gave me great satisfaction to see our tragic experience being transformed into positive and helpful experiences for others.

I immediately began exploring the many possibilities of changing my career, to work in some way within the mental health field. I even tried going back to school while I was teaching, but nothing seemed to materialize. Every avenue ended in disappointment for me. After two years of struggling, I resolved to let go of the search, and to continue teaching music and volunteering anywhere I could be of help. However, a few months later, a door was opened for me.

My school district was growing very quickly, and I was told that I needed to change from part-time teaching to full-time teaching. I had taught part-time for eight years, and because doing so had been perfect for my lifestyle, I promptly began another new job search. During this search, another school district asked if I would be interested in working part-time with music as therapy for emotionally disturbed students. They had never had this program before, and wanted to know if I would be a pioneer in that position for them. The opportunity was like a dream come true for me. I immediately knew why all the previous job possibilities had not worked out. I felt so blessed to have the chance to not only work with these special children and youth, but to share with them from the standpoint of my music background. I do not think it is a coincidence that music is a helpful healing source for mental health.

The butterfly has to struggle hard to get out of the chrysalis and become a beautiful creature in our world. I hope that my career's metamorphosis has led me to this point in my life so that I can help others feel more of the beauty that is inside them and throughout our world. I want to continually work hand-in-hand with professionals in the mental health field, to do whatever I can personally to help lessen the pain of depression, and much more.

I know my passion for helping prevent suicide will always be challenging, but I also have faith that I will continue to be blessed for the sake of others. My family and friends are pleased for me and supportive. I also feel certain that Ryan is pleased, and will continue to be near me in spirit, as he has been since his death.

Photo by Dr. Gary Noel Ross

My Confirmation Butterfly

Larry and I were asked to be guest ministers at a church campground in California for a week in July of 2002. Larry's first day of preaching turned out to be another beautiful butterfly blessing for us.

The setting was an outdoor arena set in huge trees on a mountaintop. About ten minutes into Larry's sermon, he lovingly spoke of Ryan for just about a minute, then moved on to build and conclude his message. An orange butterfly fluttered in from the left side of the stage and passed in front of Larry as he began talking about Ryan. It briefly fluttered to the right side of the stage, and flew away in the direction from which it had come as Larry finished talking about Ryan. It was perfect timing. There were no other butterflies during the service.

When Larry sat down, the congregation began singing a hymn. A friend of ours came to my side with tears in his eyes. He whispered gently, "Did you see the butterfly on stage when Larry spoke about Ryan?" I smiled and said, "I sure did!" He then paused and said, "I've heard your butterfly experiences, but this is the first time I have witnessed one with you." We knew neither of us would ever forget that orange butterfly experience. It was another confirmation for me of our many special blessings from God's precious butterflies.

Out of the Darkness

While leafing through a Newsweek magazine in January of 2002, Larry stopped on a page that mentioned suicide. He immediately called me to his side to read along with him. It advertised the first national walk for the American Foundation of Suicide Prevention. In most circumstances, we would have simply sent a contribution. But when we read the dates, we knew that we had to actively take part.

The 26-mile walk was to begin in Annandale, Virginia at dusk on August 17, the anniversary of Ryan's death. It was to end the next morning at the Washington monument in Washington, D.C. The walk was appropriately called "Out of the Darkness."

I had been diagnosed with fibromyalgia two years before, and didn't have the energy to make myself exercise during those two years. Neither Larry nor I had ever walked such a distance, but now we both had the passion. We trained hard for the long walk. I was feeling better as a result of the walking, and had Ryan to thank for that. Larry and I were very excited about participating in Ryan's memory. We knew the funds we raised from our loving family and friends would certainly help the Foundation assist others with the stigma and endless pain of depression.

The walk itself was an incredible experience for Larry and me. We both walked the entire 26 miles, and will never forget the event as long as we live. We met a lot of remarkable people, many of whom had experienced much of the same kind of loss and grieving as we had. Roughly 2,500 people participated, and we were all proud to honor our loved ones in this special way. The pain we endured to complete the 12-hour walk was nothing compared to the pain our loved ones had endured during their lives. It was a healing experience to share our stories as we walked together, out of the darkness.

At the end of the walk, Larry and I returned to our room to prepare to go home. It didn't surprise us at all when we were blessed by seeing two beautiful butterflies on a bush near our room door. We knew immediately they were sent to us from our precious and beloved Ryan. Our bodies were tired, but our hearts soared.

On October 16, 2005, friends and four generations of my family participated in a 2.5-mile "Out of the Darkness" walk in Kansas City for the Foundation. It was a powerful experience filled with memories that we will always treasure. I think Ryan was walking right along with us!

Epilogue

We are so thankful that we were blessed by having Ryan in our lives for as long as we did, even though we wish it would have been longer. I am reminded of a touching Hallmark sympathy card sent to us a few days after Ryan's death:

"A butterfly lights beside us like a sunbeam.
And for a brief moment its glory and beauty
belong to our world.
But then it flies on again, and though we wish
it could have stayed, we feel so lucky
to have seen it."

Everyone grieves the loss of loved ones in different ways, and we all have our own stories to tell. We feel so fortunate that Ryan's life continually blesses our family. May God continue to bless us all through our own healing experiences of peace, love and hope.

Recognizing Depression (from AFSP)

If a friend or loved one has a depressed mood, has lost interest or pleasure in their usual activities, and has at least five of the following symptoms for at least two weeks, they are depressed:
- Change in sleeping patterns
- Change in appetite or weight
- Speaking or moving with unusual speed or slowness
- Decrease in sexual drive
- Fatigue or loss of energy
- Feelings of worthlessness, self-reproach or guilt
- Diminished ability to concentrate, slowed thinking or indecisiveness
- Diminished ability to function
- Feelings of being out of control
- Speaking of death or suicide

Friends and loved ones are at a heightened risk of suicide when their depression is accompanied by:
- Feelings of hopelessness and desperation
- Extreme anxiety, agitation or enraged behavior
- Severe insomnia
- Increased alcohol and/or drug use

Larry and I hand out this card when we teach suicide prevention:
(The back side gives some of the important warning signs.)

HELP PREVENT SUICIDE

Ask direct questions
Listen with care
Take all threats seriously
Don't promise secrecy
Call minister, teacher, coach, counselor, or parent
FOR IMMEDIATE HELP: 1-800-SUICIDE

In loving memory of Ryan John Norris

For more details, go to the website of the American Foundation of Suicide Prevention at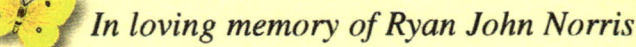
www.afsp.org/about/whattodo.htm

Made in the USA